ANOINTED

to Suffer

An Intense Journey of Spiritual Survival

Tamisha McQueen

Thea Harris Publishing, Inc.
Port St Lucie, Florida

Cover Design © 2019 by Nate Watson
Cover Art by Jessica Canegata

Published by Thea Harris Publishing * P.O. Box 7576
Port St. Lucie, FL 34985 * www.theaharris.com.
Copyright © 2019 Tamisha McQueen
All rights reserved.

ISBN- 13: 978-0-9909170-3-8

DEDICATION

This book is dedicated to broken women who have lost hope in themselves. You may be hurting now, but you will heal. I want to encourage, inspire and redirect you. The woman inside you is waiting to become the person she was always destined to be.

Tamisha

CONTENTS

ACKNOWLEDGMENTS

I am grateful for my husband, who has been by my side through the trials, tribulations, and sacrifices. His patience helped me depend on God more and our journey caused me to see life differently.

My precious Rhiley, you are my biggest blessing and the joy of my heart. I am blessed and thankful God honored me by allowing me to give birth to someone so strong and heavily anointed. I love you. You gave me the drive and determination to fight every day, my precious, Rhi Pie.

My parents for giving me life and allowing God to use them to birth something beautiful. Mother, you are a strong woman, despite the odds, you continue to press on and I admire that. Pops, you know me better than anyone because I am "you." You have *always* believed in me and your investment in me will never be forgotten.

To my former Pastor Reverend L. F. Camel and his beautiful wife First Lady Camel, thank you for guiding and mentoring me for this great ministry work. To the Bethel Missionary Church family and Youth Director, Mrs. Doris Corde and all my youth (babies), thank you for believing in me.

Rose Marie Man and Daya Chapman, my spiritual mother and sister, you powerhouses stirred up my gift, spiritually. You saw what I found hard to see in myself and poured into me when I needed it most. You are mighty women of God and I can't wait to see what He has in store for you.

My Clydina (Bonnie and Clydina) Avis Boswell. You are my sister in Christ, and I love you so much. Our hour-long phone calls, "Cheesecake Factory" outings, and transparency have been Godsent.

Last but not least, my childhood friend Chaka Cope, you were there from the beginning. You know me better than almost anyone and accepted me. I never had to question your motives. Good friends are hard to come by and I am blessed to have a friend in you.

Douglas Park and Deans Court, thank you for all your support. With hard work and dedication, we *will* continue to see our communities thrive and achieve ***greatness***!

Preface

What do you need to let go of? Who do you need to remove from your circle? Are you in the processing season of your life? If so, take a moment to listen to God's voice. What is He saying to you? You are valuable to Him. What He has promised you will come to pass. If you give your burdens to Him, you will find peace. It won't necessarily be easy, but if you continue to walk with Him, He'll help you through it.

Use *Anointed to Suffer* to identify areas where you need healing. There is liberty in getting real with yourself. I challenge you to cry before the Lord. Release every dead weight, pain, hurt, insecurity, fear and regret you have been feeling. By the time you finish reading, I pray you have freedom.

I am more concerned with your destiny than I am about you knowing my story. If you heal from what can destroy your future, you will confidently walk into that future. There is absolutely nothing we can do about our past, but we can change our future. Don't dwell on past defeats.

Do you know God allows the enemy to challenge His children? Yes, you heard me right. The enemy can't do anything to us unless He allows it. Once we truly understand we can walk in peace. We are stronger than we think.

If you are in a season of intense discomfort, you have grabbed the right book. As you read, allow God to speak to your hurt. Be prepared to transition into purpose. Your pain is only preparation for something wonderful.

I was in labor for fifty-four hours with my daughter, Rhiley. My entire body hurt as my baby positioned herself to be born. There was no relief until the last six hours when an epidural was administered. Even then, I still hurt. How can the process of giving birth be so beautiful, yet so painful?

Pregnancy sometimes includes stretch marks; I call them battle wounds. Your womb becomes enlarged as the baby grows, but it contracts to normal size after birth. Your weight also reduces, but only if you change your diet and exercise. It's possible to carry around extra pounds for years if you don't.

I experienced excruciating spiritual labor pains as I wrote this book. On October 19th, 2014, I visited my spiritual mother. I'd cried my eyes out the night before and the bags under them told the story. It was obvious I needed encouragement. While there, her son spoke powerful words to me; "Be quiet and start over." Those five words changed my life. They lifted a burden, and at that moment, I decided I would never again be defeated.

Many women fail to reach their fullest potential because their spiritual babies miscarried due to a lack of proper nutrients. My prayer is that *Anointed to Suffer* provides the revelation you need to deliver purpose. You may recognize yourself as you read the chapters. Go into your broken places and face the issues which are holding you back.

Forget everything "religion" taught you about Christian women. As you develop an intimate relationship with God, you will gain a better understanding of who you are. It's time to give birth to purpose. May *Anointed to Suffer* challenge you and take you through your journey of spiritual survival. Are you ready? Let's go! Breathe. PUSH!

Chapter One

THE PROCESS

"For I know the plan that I have for you, "declares the Lord,"
plans to prosper you and not to harm you, plans to give you hope and
a future." Jeremiah 29:11

As a little girl, I always believed I would do great things. I was going to travel the world, be the CEO of my own company, drive a fancy car and own a nice house with a pool in the backyard. I wanted to save the world. Haven't we all had those dreams? Never could I have imagined that ultimately, I would need saving.

When you're young, you don't consider misfortune, stumbling blocks, mountains, hurdles, and failures you may experience as you try to achieve your dreams. If I had known life would throw me the curveballs it did, maybe my dreams wouldn't have been so big, or maybe I would have dreamed even bigger. There is a cliché which says, *the bigger you are, the harder you fall*. I hope my falls and shortcomings are an indication of the big dreams that will eventually manifest.

God sure has a funny sense of humor. He's gotten a good laugh at me and lately, and I've joined Him. If my younger self could have foreseen what she would go through to get to those dreams, would she have been willing to do whatever it took to see those dreams come to fruition? She didn't anticipate the process.

It all began early in 2011. My life was going in the direction I envisioned. My husband and I had upgraded to a 1,100 sq. ft. Condo. My marriage was great. I was an aspiring Realtor and everything I worked hard for was falling into place. However, in the midst of it all, it was clear my plans did not align with God's. He TERMINATED them at the height of what I called my success.

It took years, and though God was trying to get my attention, I did not recognize His voice.

If someone told me the life I was trying to create for my family would come crashing down months later, I would have said they were delusional; not my life, but I had to be realistic. My real estate deals were delayed, consistently canceled, or someone kept outbidding my client's offers. In an office full of ambitious people, my confidence started to match my inability to make a sale. In the game of real estate, if you don't move your feet, you don't eat. Of course, it is typical for a few deals to fail, but almost every deal? I could not catch a break. It took years, and though God was trying to get my attention, I did not recognize His voice. My hunger for personal gain had gotten in the way of hearing the Lord's voice.

On June 6th of the same year, I was hit with a double whammy. I was pregnant, and we were now struggling financially. We'd been married for ten years with no children. I should have been rejoicing. Instead, I was so stressed out I couldn't even celebrate the life we were about to bring into this world. My greatest fear was upon me.

Our debt to income ratio was through the roof. My husband's hours were cut due to a lack of inventory during the slow summer months and my deals weren't going through. More bad news came, because my due date was after the health insurance enrollment period, we had to pay the first three thousand dollars out of pocket to give birth to our daughter. Where would we get the money? What my husband and I were earning was less than we needed to pay our bills.

We paid six hundred dollars a month for family medical insurance premiums. With an upgraded lifestyle, we were now faced with restricted cash flow and more unforeseen expenses. I felt like God was failing me. Where had I gone wrong? I paid my tithes, went to church, lived right and was not bothering anybody. I always thought if you did good, good would always follow you. My mind shifted, there was no God and those who preached the gospel, I avoided. If there was a God I wouldn't be going through this struggle. Why are the bad blessed and the good cursed? I gave up on God.

**To be honest; I never thought I was good
enough for God to talk to me. That's
what religion taught me.**

I stopped going to church and spent the next eight months of my pregnancy confined and depressed. If God was not going to see about me, I was not going to serve Him. At that time in my life, I was not yet in an intimate relationship with Him. I didn't have the right mindset to recognize the season. I'd forgotten, at the beginning of the year, God told me to pray and read the Bible more because He wanted a deeper relationship with me. I dismissed it, too busy with all I was trying to do in my life. My inability to obey His instructions caused the next few years of pain. Had I been more intimate with God, I would have known

He was warning me of what was to come. His instructions were to prepare me for the journey ahead. I was angry for the entire year of my trial. To be honest, I never thought I was good enough for God to talk to me, that's what religion taught me. Besides, how could I know God's voice when I was so full of pride?

Separation and devastation often come before God elevates you. Little did I know, God was about to use my insecurities, fears, hurts, and pain to birth something new. It was time to take out the spiritual, mental and emotional trash. I had years of garbage for Him to sort out. It wasn't until I got out of my emotions that I started to understand God's purpose. I could see what He was doing through my pain; He took me deeper into places that were dormant for a long time. I was in the position He needed me to be in to properly hear His voice. What a blessing to know; I had not chosen God, He'd chosen me.

I'd been running from Him for years, on a reckless mission to be somebody, to prove people wrong about me and prove myself right. God was never in the equation. Although I was living a *good Christian life* and strived for the *American dream*, my motives were all wrong. I wasn't for a good life for my family, I was trying to please people. I wanted to create a life the people who caused me so much pain would envy and be constantly reminded of my success. The only thing I thought of was getting revenge for the pain I experienced.

I wanted to create a life the people who caused me so much pain would envy and be constantly reminded of my success.

The more I tried to prove myself, the more I looked like the fool. Everything my hands touched crumbled. I was no longer in control, and I was used to having control. I had my first job at age fourteen, and my own place by eighteen. I knew how to take care of Tamisha. Was I really going to trust God to take care of me? Where was He when my childhood was stripped from me? Where was He when I longed to be able to have a normal upbringing?

Most of my life, I tried to *become* what some called "a jack of all trades and a master of none." Not boasting but I probably have more credentials than a person twice my age. Uncle Sam and my student loans can attest to that, which is a whole testimony. Don't get me wrong though, I made money and had fun, but the reality was, I was heading for burnout. I was obsessed with people's perception of me. As I tried to show them, I moved further and further away from God's plans for me. He was patient with me though, He knew I would eventually get tired of running. Sadly, those I was trying to impress were doing worse than I was.

"If I spent that much energy *in* God rather than on the opinions of people suffering from their own insecurities, I would have been walking in His purpose a long time ago.

Every year I wanted to be something else. I never committed to anything long enough for it to grow. I became bored when I didn't get the results I wanted, as fast as I wanted them. The one thing I was sure of was that I would be my own boss. I had the resources, the tenacity, and the support, but I didn't focus on what my heart was saying. Those were the most tormented years of my life. God kept talking to me, but I was too busy and too stubborn. Let me keep it real, I didn't want to do what He was asking. I just wanted to live, my way!

When I finally, for the first time, made a full commitment to something, God said, "No." I didn't want to hear anything if it wasn't what I wanted to do. I was focused on my real estate career, trying to become the It Girl, a top luxury real estate agent, the empire builder, the BOSS. The only thing that seemed positive then was my financial status. It would have destroyed the plans God had for me. I am certain about this because I had all the right ideas, but the wrong motivation. There was no doubt I would reach every goal, yet I still have the same insecurities and mindset. I would have self-destructed. I had to face my issues. What God had for me did not include impressing people. It was time to impress Him.

Sometimes we bring the wrath of God into our lives when we walk in disobedience. He was merciful, yet I fought Him. If I spent that much energy *in* God rather than on the opinions of people suffering from their own insecurities, I would have been walking in His purpose a long time ago. God was tired of me wasting my life. He loved me so much, He cut my shenanigans short.

We better stop giving the enemy accolades for our own foolishness. Satan was not laughing with me; he was laughing at me. I was a fool. He didn't have to destroy me; He was watching me destroy myself. There are just some things we cause. My life was reckless. God wanted me to end the nonsense. He couldn't allow me to continue to live a lie.

"For what does it profit a man, if he gains the whole world, and forfeits his soul?" Mark 8:36

Through pain, God released my biggest breakthroughs. I can remember tearfully asking my husband, "Why am I going through so much?" He said, "You asked for this." I could not believe those words came out of his mouth. It felt like a double-edged sword had sliced me open. I needed words of encouragement, and he was rubbing salt into my open wounds.

As much as I wanted to deny it, he was right. He then reminded me about what I'd petitioned God for in October of the previous year. I asked Him to do a new thing in me; I wanted more of Him. He was giving me what I asked for; it just didn't come in the pretty decorated package I wanted. I didn't recognize I was in a process. I was being purged and refined. The pressure would become greater. There was so much junk in my heart, God had to do major reconstruction. It was only by His grace I was not committed to a mental institution during that season.

Joyce Meyer said it best in the title of one of her books, "The battlefield is in the mind." Most of us are defeated because we don't understand what we are fighting. I felt more pain and dealt with more issues walking with God than when I was walking in my own deceit. Imagine that. I was in the fight of my life. This fight forced me to deal with my problems, and each blow knocked down a different wall of issues. I was too consumed with a false self-image to deal with the things which held me back.

The mind is powerful. Left in despair for too long, it can destroy you, especially if your heart is also deceived. Major damage control was needed. Both my heart and mind had years of garbage, thirty years of bad habits and deep-rooted emotions stored up over time. It would take more than a couple of kumbaya sessions to get rid of them. I needed deliverance!!

If the enemy can flood your mind, he will overtake you. Let's just say I had been hoodwinked and bamboozled. Almost everything I imagined was false. I was a pawn in his game. Don't feel sorry for me though, God had a plan.

"But as for you, ye thought evil against me; but
God meant it unto good, to bring to pass, as it is
this day, to save much people alive."
Genesis 50:20

I needed to go through to step into His purpose. He had to

take everything I had to get me to a place where He could deal with me. I was stripped down to nothing with no security net to catch me. In my pain and despair, I began to see what was real. It's unfortunate it took that valley to show me I was the one who'd caused it.

Lean your spiritual ear to me for a minute. Forget everything religion taught you. When we are guided by our carnal (natural) mind, we often become distracted by what is going on in the world. Our focus is not on God, but on our own strengths and abilities. Carnality deceives. It's where Satan lives, waiting to devour. Oh, but in the valley, the place of our breaking, we get our biggest blessing. It is there God begins to train our spiritual ear to hear Him. My valley experience brought me major blessings, and my Job trials became my greatest deliverance. It is a place of our deepest revelation, where we develop a relationship with God.

It was three years before I was out of that pit. I was depressed, felt unworthy, and defeated, all because of rejection and pain. In my weakness, God's strength and grace helped me. There were times when I wanted to give up, to be honest, there were times I did. However, God did not let me stay in despair. Like Jonah, the "whale" spit me out (Jonah 2:10).

If you are in your own *process*, don't fight it. Allow God to minister to you. The more I fought, the longer I stayed in my pain. There is power in surrendering all your burdens and troubles to the Lord. If you want to experience a peace which surpasses all understanding, quit fighting and allow God to do what He does best - fight your battles. Write down every struggle, hurt, pain, brokenness, burdened relationship, insecurity, and bondage. Be one hundred percent honest with God and release them. Rest. There is a purpose for your life. Once the purging process is over, you will come out as pure gold. It is time to let go.

God knew I would go through trouble for His glory and kingdom building. During my tribulation, I spent time in prayer seeking answers from Him. Prayer changes things. Develop a prayer life, and watch God. He will equip you to handle all the challenges you face. Pray this prayer of deliverance.

Deliverance Prayer

Heavenly Father, guide the women reading this book. Allow it to minister to their spirit. You are the Father of hope and love. Through You, deliverance and peace flow from a river of living water that cleanses and purifies. Touch every dead place in their lives and breathe fresh life into every situation that has caused them to be barren. Renew their hearts and impregnate them with fresh purpose and an anointing to break every yoke and destroy all the chains in their lives. Clear their minds and hearts and replace them with Your love. Your love delivers. Break every stronghold and bondage. Build their confidence so they can see You, so they may know who You have called them to be and not what the enemy has told them. We bind every generational curse, the spirit of rejection, abandonment, feelings of inadequacies, depression, oppression, addictions, unworthiness, debt, defeat, loneliness, molestation, and fear as You clear their minds of anything not like You. We agree today. All these things we pray in Jesus' name.
Amen!

Exercise 1

There is power in letting go. Only then can God work, only then are you healed. Take a few moments and list the things you want to let go.

1._____

_____

_____

_____

_____

2._____

_____

_____

_____

_____

3._____

_____

_____

_____

_____

_____

_____

4._____

_____

_____

_____

_____

_____

5._____

_____

_____

_____

_____

_____

Chapter Two

A SEED WAS PLANTED

"The enemy planted the seed of rejection at birth and it grew over the next thirty-two years."

Let's look at the history of trees. Have you ever wondered about their origin? According to the Guinness Book of World Records, the tallest known living tree in the world is the Redwood Hyperion, also known as the Sequoia. It is in Northern California. The Hyperion measures up to 380 feet and is believed to be between 700 to 800 years old.[1] How amazing this large tree came from such a small seed.

Once a seed is planted, it takes deep root in fertile ground and intertwines with the other roots around it, the same way the seeds in our lives, good and bad, are planted. What have you allowed to creep into your garden? Some of us let the pain of our childhood take root and spread. Unless you can get the seed out before it takes root, just like the Sequoia, it will continue to grow.

Are you ready to meet my younger self? My roots run deep. There were multiple seeds attached to them. Raised in the small town of Okeechobee, Florida, I was privileged to be nurtured by my grandmother, the late Catherine Cummings. She loved me dearly. I couldn't have asked for a better childhood. Mrs. "Cat," as she was called, was a large woman in stature, and greatly known for her cooking. If you lived in the Douglas Park community, you knew Mrs. Cat. Although she was not my biological grandmother (she was married to my Grandfather), her love never reflected it. Cat protected me, and I protected her. I can still hear her yelling, "Misha, bring your tail in this house," and that was the clean version. I think of her constantly, and believe she is dancing with my guarding angel.

I am a product of two teen parents (well one known for sure at least). At the time, I was Momma's baby, but Daddy's maybe. My mother was fifteen years old when she gave birth to me, and the alleged father was on his way to college. Like most parents of promising athletic teen-aged boys, his parents wanted what was best for their son. They did what they thought would protect his future. Besides, in the eyes of some, my mother was fast (as the old folks would say). People wondered if she warranted respect and questioned whether her daughter deserved to have a father in her life. I was headed toward a painful journey I would have to face alone. The enemy planted the seed of rejection at birth and it grew over the next thirty-two years. Although I now have a loving relationship with both of my parents, it took much prayer and healing to get there.

"But while men slept, his enemy came and sowed
tares among the wheat, and went his way."
Mathew 13:25

My pain did not surface until after my Grandmother died. Her death broke me, and part of me died with her. The enemy waited patiently. He watered the seeds planted as early as my conception. Rejection, abandonment, and insecurity began to take deeper root at a massive speed. What once lay dormant manifested. Those seeds kept producing a harvest that affected me for years.

The devil's biggest upper hand is our inability to recognize the seeds he plants. They only grow if they're watered and fed. It's how the enemy creates strongholds. Thoughts, bad experiences, hurts, and unforgiveness are the water. We don't recognize it, but once planted, if they're not properly destroyed, the roots go deep. There is no visible sign it's growing at first. It waits for an opportunity to present itself.

Pain and disappointment also water the seed. Before you know it, you have harvested a garden of bitterness, envy, and malice. These bad seeds which produce weeds grow with the plants trying to develop greatness in your life. If you don't get rid of them, they shelter insects and infections and kill fruit-producing flowers. They come to choke the life out of the fruit in your garden. Weeds grow quickly and overtake plants. They are toxic! If you want to protect your garden, you must dig up weeds from the root.

I didn't get rid of rejection. It was watered during an experience when I was ten. I went nearby to a friend's house to play with her. She had company. Her guest's oldest sister met me about five feet from her doorstep. She greeted me with, "they don't want to play with you," and then began telling me the reasons why. Her words hurt. They must have spotted me well before I had gotten to the house. I was not the most attractive ten-year-old. They were pretty. Picture a chubby girl with a jerry curl, known to walk the streets barefoot, who looked like a tomboy. Other girls envied these girls. I was rejected by them.

The walk back home was cold. I remember feeling depressed; a memory which stayed with me until I forgave her twenty-three years later. Those words had a long-lasting effect on my relationship with that young lady and many others who have been part of my life since then. I became guarded and immediately suspected any woman who had the same traits she'd exhibited at the time. One traumatic moment in my life, yet a key reminder of how easy it is for negative seeds to take over our garden. I had to release her and the residue those weeds produced.

Many years later, I reconnected with her and confronted the issue, one I didn't know would have such a negative impact on me. At the time, twelve years had passed, but I still held her accountable. God showed me how my negative perception of her grew because of false images I'd created of her. Even if she is reading this book right now, she may not even know how she affected my life. People move on and we are stuck. I forgave her for what she said, and myself for carrying that burden, and began to heal from the encounter. Unfortunately, I had many more seeds to dig up.

The greatest trick the devil ever pulled was convincing the world he doesn't exist. Wesley Snipes said it and it's true. Satan is strategic, he is a great manipulator. He is also patient; he doesn't mind waiting for the seeds he plants to grow. His victory comes after the seed matures, especially if we are not aware it is in our garden. How can you defeat something you don't know exists?

Perhaps we suffered from the same seed; she wasn't raised by her mother either.

I had a wonderful childhood with Ms. Cat and never thought about being parentless until she died. For the first twelve years of my life; *she* was my mother. I was sure of Ms. Cat's love, but she didn't fill the void caused by my mother's abandonment. After her death, it felt like I was serving a prison sentence. I was chained to a mental prison for the next twenty years. My only protector was gone.

I left a town I had known all my life to move over 500 miles away to Atlanta. I was exposed, naked and vulnerable, forced to live with my biological mother, a woman who didn't know me. I felt like a foreigner. She loved me, but there was no motherly bond. The problem wasn't because my mother hadn't raised me to that point, it was our relationship after she got her opportunity. For years, I tried to gain her acceptance and it was met with more rejection and pain. She couldn't love me like I needed her to, and I didn't understand why. Perhaps we suffered from the same seeds; she wasn't raised by her mother either.

For years I couldn't understand it. Did she grow up feeling the way I did? Did she ever crave her mother's love? Maybe she internalized her childhood suffering differently. One thing I knew for certain, I'd inherited the seed. It was ancient, generational, and determined to stay because it was a curse. My mother and I were two of a kind, living life with the same outcomes. It was Deja vu for her, but a constant reality for me, one that took years to heal.

I looked like my mother and her mother. As I grew older, I understood they were victims too. We were connected by a four-generation curse which caused much hurt in our lives. One of my dear friends in the ministry told me, "the enemy has no new tricks." He capitalizes on our pitfalls, and unless they are found and corrected, we pass them on to our children. The seed replenishes itself and takes deeper root. I was determined not to allow it into the lives of my future children.

I wanted a child, but I was afraid.

My husband and I were married for ten years before we welcomed our first child, though it was not our first pregnancy. We'd miscarried in the first year of marriage. I struggled with that loss for a great while and questioned whether I would ever be able to have children. It hardened an already damaged heart. There was an inward battle. I wanted a child but was afraid I couldn't handle another loss. Maybe it was for the best. If I didn't have any children, it would spare them the pain I had experienced.

I selfishly and purposely denied my husband children because I was afraid to repeat the cycle. For years I was content without kids. I traveled, enjoying the freedom of not having to care for anyone but myself. The older I got, the more I convinced myself to be satisfied with never becoming a parent. The scary part about it all is, I was truly happy. My husband seemed to have come to that conclusion too. He stopped asking, and it was fine with me.

Deep down inside, I did want to experience motherhood someday, but it constantly reminded me of my past. Would I continue the generational cycle? I was too afraid I would never have a bond with my children. I couldn't give them something that was foreign to me. I'd rather spare them the heartache. I wasn't sure I had the capacity to love a child when I was emotionally unable to properly love myself. My fears and insecurities deprived my husband of fatherhood.

When I found out I was pregnant, I prayed for a little boy. Maybe then I wouldn't have to deal with the issues that plagued the women in my family. I was adamant about not destroying some little girl's life. The thought of having a daughter was devastating. I can still remember the day the ultrasound tech told me I was having a little girl. I cried. All I could think of was not being able to love her the way she needed, not being able to connect with her, and messing up her life. I was already depressed during my pregnancy and this increased it.

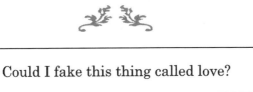

Could I fake this thing called love?

Unknowingly, it had already started. My daughter wasn't even here yet and my relationship with her was already being affected. The seed was trying to take root. I was detached, watering the seed of rejection for the life growing inside me. When I gave birth and the doctor placed my daughter, Rhiley, on my chest, there was absolutely no connection. No happy tears flowed. My heart didn't palpitate. The only question I asked was,

"Does she have any hair?" I was trying to keep it together because my mother-in-law was in the room. How could I carry someone so precious inside of me for nine months and not become attached? I felt inhumane. Perhaps it was because my whole world had also crumbled when I was born. Whatever it was, I could see myself slipping into a familiar situation. What was wrong with me? Was I a monster? What would I do now? I had a baby I was unsure I could love and a husband who always wanted a little girl. Could I fake this thing called love?

"The prayers of the righteous availed much" (James 5:16) and God heard my heartfelt prayers. In spite of the fact I convinced myself I had no desire to have children, I always prayed over my womb. I prayed the iniquities of mine and my husband's forefathers would not attach themselves to my offspring. God agreed with my petition because He confirmed it. My prayers reversed the generational curse over my children's lives.

Hours after Rhiley's birth, the nurse showed me how to properly breastfeed her. When her big eyes rested upon my face something sparked, I knew I would never, and could never do anything to hurt her. I was determined to give her the life she deserved. She was precious and literally a miracle.

God had given her to us (He sent a man of God to prophesy her arrival and confirmed it through my husband's aunt). Rhiley was special, and God entrusted her to me. The deeply rooted seed was gone, and it all began with the birth of my daughter. The spirit of rejection was deprived of nourishment.

Rhiley gave me the strength to fight for us. Her birth was the beginning of many breakthroughs, but I was not in the clear yet. I had a long way to go before being completely healed. God revealed what seeds were planted and what had to be done to uproot them. It took me years to accept the Lord was the only one who could help me. I was fighting myself and an enemy I didn't recognize.

You can't heal the wounds you cover up.

God allowed the worst season of my life. I held the keys to unlock my future and he was about to show me how to do it. It was He who gave the enemy permission to shake me, push me and even tear me down. He allowed it because He knew I was tough enough to handle it. God's plan for my life was much greater than the pain I was experiencing. Pain builds character, patience, and endurance. I had to confront those issues in my life that beat me down, mocked me, and scared me. God was preparing me for what was to come.

You can't heal the wounds you cover up. Are you ready to tackle those issues? If so, confront the little girl who has been molested, rejected, neglected, abandoned and hurt by her parents. Confront the teenager who was raped, abused, and humiliated by her peers. Confront the broken woman who was betrayed, lied to and lied on by a friend or relative. Confront the woman who was mentally, physically and emotionally abused by a cheating husband or boyfriend. I know it hurts, but freedom comes through that pain.

There are so many families who won't face issues. If we are honest with ourselves, a lot of our traits come from our parents. You're in debt, your parents are in debt. You struggle in your relationships, so do your parents. How is your temper? Let me guess, your parents or grandparents have the same temper too? Whatever the issue, you got it from somewhere. If not from a parent, then from another ancestor. Challenge yourself about those lingering feelings that have kept you in bondage for so long. After you've looked at the issues stunting your growth, forgive those who wronged you and forgive yourself! You are not defined by your circumstances. CONFRONT and FORGIVE so God can RELEASE you into destiny. Allow Him to restore you. You are entering a season of restoration and unprecedented peace.

Deliverance Prayer

Father God, I am coming to You broken and in need. Wrap your arms around me. You know the issues that have plagued me. Lead me to all truth and give me the grace to deal with the seed(s) that have been planted in my life. I have been letting my past interfere with my future. Here is my brokenness. I release everything and everyone that has broken it. Lord, free me from shame, embarrassment, and condemnation. I am whole in You and I declare completer freedom and victory over my life. Create a new heart in me and renew my mind. I am not the seed(s) that were planted, and they will not affect my children or their children. All these things I pray in Jesus name Amen!

Exercise 2

What seeds have you allowed to hinder your growth and keep you from your destiny? It is time to identify, confront and be released from them. Get to the root.

1._____

_____

_____

_____

_____

_____

2._____

_____

_____

_____

_____

3.

4.

5.

Chapter Three

MISUNDERSTOOD

Trying to force people to understand you or your goals may cause them to resent you. I figured this out, painfully. Be careful, you unknowingly shed light on areas in their lives that lack vision. Those who lack vision will never understand the dreams and ideas God gives to you. You secretly become the enemy, unintentionally stirring their insecurities. People will misjudge what they don't understand. They say, "She thinks she knows it all" "There she goes again with another idea." I never meant any harm. I was just being Tamisha. I've always had a big personality. Extra is how some describe it. If being me was extra, then I was the most extra person I knew. Despite everything I had gone through, I always kept a smile on my face. Whether I felt like it or not, I had to keep my composure. People were watching. Unfortunately, not always in a good way.

It was my mission to see the best in people and do anything to help. How could that be misunderstood? I never wanted people to go through what I had gone through, so I overcompensated by trying to pull the best out of everyone. Perhaps I was being too positive or expected too much. When people have a problem with themselves it eventually affects how they choose to see you.

As far back as I can remember, there was a false perception of me. I always felt I had to defend what I said or clarify what I really meant. I know we are not all going to get along. Every personality won't mesh, but these were people I never even had a conversation with. Geesh! No wonder I stayed so confused. I couldn't keep up with all the drama I caused by just being me. It had gotten to a point where living as Tamisha was no longer fun. I finally convinced myself I was always the problem because I was trying to attach myself to the wrong people. I wanted them to accept me. Surely, I was the one who needed to change.

It felt like I was in a twilight zone. The more people misunderstood me the more I wanted to be attached to them. I will make them understand me, I thought. If only I could get them to see who I really was. I constantly relived my childhood need to be accepted at any cost. I spent many hours in my shower curled up in the fetal position, crying and wondering why people just could not get me. Why wasn't I liked? What did I do to them? I tortured myself for many years believing the things that were said about me. Was I the problem, did I really think I was better than others? This thinking contradicted how I treated people. I always put them first. Maybe that was my problem and often my demise, being so consumed by what others thought, I did not value myself.

The word says, it is the anointing that breaks the yoke (Isaiah 10:27), and it was evident she was the anointed vessel God sent to minister to me.

I eventually learned I was largely misunderstood because I didn't know who I was. I was as much a wonder to myself as I was to others. Looking back, I don't think they had found themselves yet either. One thing was certain, I could no longer deal with the hurt that came with it. I was so tired of trying to prove myself, loving people who didn't want to love me back. Up came those childhood issues again. I tried to get people to see me for who I was, they painted a picture of who they thought I was. It hurt to be myself as much as it hurt trying to keep up with what people wanted or thought I should be.

I spent pointless years trying to prove I was somebody no matter what people thought and ran away from my calling. Could it be those I was trying to impress were really trying to impress me? It took a long time to see how deep their infliction of pain ran. Lord knows I toiled trying to find myself. I was tired. It seemed like an endless journey. I was already who God said I was, I just hadn't accepted it. I allowed other's opinions to keep me from seeing me.

One spring evening I had an encounter with a true woman of God who I'd met on social media. It was an appointed assignment that changed how I viewed myself forever. The exchange spoke directly to the stronghold in my life. She inboxed a four-word message, "You are good enough." It freed me from the lies I believed. Those words broke years of bondage. I cried. With every tear, a layer of insecurity, pain and hurt rolled with it. The Holy Spirit lit a flame. The enemy no longer held me. Healing and deliverance had begun. The word says, "It is the anointing that breaks the yoke" (Isaiah 10:27). It was evident she was the anointed vessel God sent to minister to me.

For years I wrestled with feelings of inadequacy. I didn't think God used people like me, only those who had it all together. It was clear I didn't read my Bible regularly during that season because the good Book consists of many flawed individuals who God used to do mighty things. Church folks let's stop making people feel they have to be perfect to be received by God. We have unrealistic expectations of them when we are flawed too.

It was if God gave me a brand-new pair of eyes and ears. My mind began to align with the thoughts God had toward me. I had never felt like this before. He loved me and accepted me even if no one else did. I was His beloved! This freedom felt good. It was foreign and exciting. I had self-esteem. Whew! It was over, I was about to take over the world, and never be hurt again. I had arrived. Now I could walk into the purpose God had for me, right? He answered, "Of course not, this is only the surface of what I have begun in you." There were more layers to be removed, but now I had the strength and the security to see it to the end. The journey wouldn't be easier, but my confidence was ready for what was ahead. I was God-confident now. He needed me to understand I was good enough before He could continue to mold me for where I was going. There were more revelations coming and more chains needed to fall off my neck before I could walk in complete freedom.

Many of us are wrestling because we won't let God complete the work He has begun in us. We think when we've conquered one area the work is done. When God begins a work, He completes it. We determine how long the process takes. God let me see, people were supposed to misunderstand me. If that never happened, I would have gotten comfortable with some of the relationships I had and His will for me wouldn't have been accomplished. I was supposed to be rejected, abandoned, lied on talked about and criticized, an outcast. How else would I be strong enough to fight the spiritual battles that were ahead? God built me for this assignment. "If we suffer with Him, we will reign with Him" (2 Timothy 2:12).

Some of today's Christians will not reach their potential because they don't want to go through anything. Have you ever looked at a man or woman of God and thought, "Wow, they are surely anointed?" People who walk in a higher dimension of God are there because they have gone through the fire. Their willingness to do it earned them a greater reward. You see the glory of the Lord on them, but you don't see the hell they faced to get it. That's why there's a lot of jealousy in the Body of Christ. We're so concerned with other's anointings and won't allow the Lord to do what He needs to in us so we too can build His Kingdom. Salvation is free, but the anointing costs. Are you willing to be crucified for it?

Even Jesus suffered. He paid the ultimate sacrifice to sit on the right hand of the Father. He was God. He could have called a host of angels to take Him down from the cross, but He had a purpose to fulfill. His crucifixion is an example of how we may suffer. We must die to all things not like Him. I had a lot of dying to do. Everything was beginning to make sense. God never meant for me to live in bondage, I came to the realization, I needed Him. I was never meant to fit in; I was supposed to wander in the wilderness all by myself. It was there I found God's love. Being misunderstood was not so bad after all. I had one thing in common with everyone else; I'd misunderstood me too. I wasn't fighting other people; I was fighting myself. I wanted people to understand a person who didn't even understand herself.

We suffer most when we purposely ignore the will of God. He gave me divine instructions about where He wanted my life to go. I wasn't in tune enough to follow His voice. God is alive. He speaks to us, some more than others. Sometimes, we choose to ignore what the Lord is telling us. As a result, we suffer the consequences because we're outside His will, open to the enemy's attack. Although we can eventually get back on track, the journey is much longer. There is protection in the will of God!

When I stopped fighting and surrendered, revelation flowed. It was like a hundred-piece jigsaw puzzle had been scattered on the ground with God moving to put the pieces back together, pieces I allowed the enemy to divide. Each piece represented an area of great hurt. I had to deal with each one independently before I could find and connect the next one. Some were easier to fit than others, but it was still hard. It was hard to believe so many were broken. They needed Doctor Jesus. Thank God, I didn't have to face it alone.

At times, it appeared I was halfway through reconstruction, then a situation in my life would unravel some of the pieces I worked so hard to put together. I thought I was accomplishing something because it felt like smooth sailing. God showed me I had illegally connected some pieces. I wasn't cleared to move on. Sometimes, we cover up wounds and don't give them time to heal. We live with dormant issues that awaken when some situation aggravates them because we had not laid them to rest. After all the hard work, God told me to start over. He was doing the guiding this time.

The old Tamisha would bury the issue without seeking God for healing and guidance. He taught me to do just the opposite. I had to deal with them to properly heal and move on for good. If I hadn't, I would continue to be tested in the same way. However, God was patient with me. Soon, those pieces that no longer fit, were fitting perfectly. He opened my eyes and I understood what

I'd been doing wrong.

Life really is like a puzzle. You must study yourself to find the right pieces to complete the work of art. Thank God for Holy Spirit. There are some parts of us only He can put together. I think He designed it that way so we can form a greater relationship with him. I finally accepted there would be no shortcuts. I knew by instinct which pieces of my life's puzzle needed more healing time. I started paying closer attention, being particularly careful with this jigsaw puzzle. The picture it was forming would lead to my destiny; I could not rush what God was doing. He wants the best for us. To receive it, we must accept His plans for our lives.

Some of us misunderstand who we are because we have no idea who He is calling us to be. We allow people's perceptions to dictate our worth. The only opinion which matters is God's. It is important to know your purpose. When I was younger, God gave me glimpses of my future. From time to time He even showed me (in dreams) the direction He wanted me to take. It was up to me to trust Him and align myself with those plans. He loves to see His people blessed. The more we commit ourselves to Him, the more He reveals His perfect plan for our lives.

I believe God wanted to give me hope for my future. He was always with me, but because I was not in covenant with Him, I was far from His path for me. I missed His clues. The enemy knows how important we are to God and tries to keep us from an intimate relationship with Him. His job is to make sure we never reach our full potential. Why do you think he fights us so hard? You'd better check yourself when he stops. He pays attention to what triggers you. Not only because he planted the seeds, but because he spends much of his time studying your ways. He learns your personality, what upsets you and who hurts you. In order to defeat him, you must know his strategy. The only way to learn it is to connect yourself to God and His word.

A woman who understands her purpose is feared by the enemy. She is focused on her calling and is determined to get there. She walks in purpose. The enemy's job is to keep us confused and unsure of ourselves and far from our destinies. I constantly tried to reinvent myself not knowing what I was looking for. God is not the author of confusion. Once I fully surrendered and committed myself to Him, He dealt with my uncertainty and all misunderstandings I had of myself and Him. Surrender. Commit. Let God lead you. Give Him full control. You won't regret it. It was hard to fully trust God at first because I was used to regulating my own life, but I eventually did.

I gave up the temporary pleasures I thought were my heart's desires and traded them for what God wanted. It scared me because there was no way my mind could have fathomed His plans. They were so much greater. I needed God.

For the first time in my life, I was truly excited about my future. I blindly walked in the direction He had been pointing me to all along. It did not make the task easier, but it more comfortable knowing whatever happened on the journey, I would reach my destiny after all that running, and years of not knowing myself. This race was designed just for me. God knew the plans He had for me (Jeremiah 29:11).

Are you confused about who you are supposed to be? Have you reached your full potential? Give your life to God, let Him have your fears, doubts, questions, and concerns. He knows what to do with them. Take a moment to think about what He has been showing you, whether through people, things or opportunities. Stay in that place.

God always gives us little nuggets about where He is taking us to prepare us for it. We, however, stop the process by getting distracted and losing focus. Losing focus delays. When Peter took his eyes off Jesus, he began to sink, but as long as he focused on the One who was calling him into the sea, he walked on water (Matthew 14:22-23). If I move when God leads, I am fine. When I get distracted, my process is delayed. We often get sidetracked because we are impatient. Don't allow *self* to mess this up. God must get you ready. This is why He strips us of self and clothes us in Him. "How can old wine be poured into new skin," (Matthew 9:14-17).

If we are given something too soon, we will destroy it. God can't pour great destiny into a broken vessel. Little by little, it spills out and becomes useless. Don't let pride and past hurt rob you of destiny.

Deliverance Prayer

Thank you, Lord, for allowing me to see myself in Your image. You have called me to do mighty things through Your strength and power. I will continue to walk in your will. Thank You for accepting me for me when others misunderstood me. Release me from any hurt or malice toward those who caused me pain. I am who You called me to be. Give me faith to fully accept my calling and to confidently take my rightful place in it. You are my strength and peace. As I imitate You on this journey, I have full assurance You will continue to cover and guide me. I trust the plan You have for my life and fully accept that sometimes being misunderstood is Your way of protecting me.
Amen

Exercise 3

*You have to defeat the issues in your life. It is time to identify,
confront and be released from them. What are some of the seeds
planted in your life, that hurt you?*

1._____

_____

_____

_____

_____

_____

2._____

_____

_____

_____

_____

_____

3._____

_____

_____

_____

_____

_____

4._____

_____

_____

_____

_____

_____

5._____

_____

_____

_____

_____

_____

Chapter Four

ATTACHMENTS

As long as I can remember, I attached myself to toxic things - romantic relationships, friendships, and emotional eating. It was a temporary fix for my pain. I didn't value myself. I was at constant war with who I thought I was and who I wanted to become. You may have heard that opposites attract. We spend years in science classes with illustrations of gravity and the law of attraction. I remember my grade-school teacher giving a demonstration on how negative and positive ends gravitate toward one another while the two like ends repel each other. I thought it was fascinating. After many trials and errors in my personal life, the concept didn't hold much weight or value in my world.

You must be connected with like-minded people
to stir up the vision inside you.

As a child, I always felt like someone was walking with me, but I didn't know who. Other times, I felt disconnected. It was hard for my younger self to embrace who God was calling me to be. I wanted to fit in and be like the cool kids. Even though I was well known, it seemed like I was alone on an island. There were many disappointments while I was trying to find myself, some because of wrong associations.

My leader, Bishop Kenneth Williams, once made an illustration that impacted my thought process. He said, "Peter walked with Jesus, but he was not connected to Him." How could someone walk with Jesus for as long as Peter did and not know Him? As my Pastor broke it down my whole life started to make sense. I had been trying to connect myself to things and people I shouldn't be attached to (they didn't know me, not really. They knew of me, but never truly connected to who I was).

People can be attached to you, spend time with you and not even know you. Peter was with Jesus during good times and hard times, but he had internal struggles. He was at odds with Jesus, especially over His prophecy about His death. Peter's heart was right, but his faith and lack of understanding made it impossible for him to properly connect. It wasn't until Jesus died that he got it! He became a great man of God; one God chose to build His church.

Jesus and Peter's story had a happy ending, but I can't say the same for some of mine. Some people become attracted to you but will never commit. That is why so many friendships and business relationships don't last. Connect with like-minded people to stir up the vision inside you.

"When Elizabeth heard Mary's greeting, the baby leaped in her womb, and Elizabeth was filled with the Holy Spirit" (Luke 1:40). The words Mary spoke were so powerful, they caused Elizabeth's baby to leap! These women were connected for a greater purpose. They both had babies who would eventually complement each other. Their covenant produced a manifestation of the ultimate covenant, one that would save us from sin.

True covenants are for purpose.
They birth legacies.

When you are in "covenant" with the right people, the babies in your wombs appropriately respond to one another. The Greek word διαθηκη (diatheke) usually translated "covenant" in English versions of the Bible, is a legal term denoting a formal and legally binding declaration of benefits to be given by one party to another, with or without conditions attached (NIV Women's Study Bible 2015).

Be careful of the covenants you make. Your destiny is too important for you to be attached to the wrong people. Remember the two babies in Mary's and Elizabeth's stomachs? They would meet again thirty years later. One was John the Baptist who baptized Jesus, and the other was Jesus, who died for us? True covenants are for purpose. They birth legacies and produce fruit. God honors covenants.

You can't produce a harvest with just anybody. It may look good in the beginning, or sound good for a moment, but the fruit will eventually rot. I spent years entertaining wrong covenants. They were not bad people, but they were bad for me. It also could be I was bad for them.

Have you ever had to rely on your navigational system and still missed your turn? Just like the Global Positioning System (GPS), when you are going in the wrong direction, you will be redirected to the right route. God wants us to produce our best fruit. Opposites don't always attract. Life taught me that. If we are not connected to the right people, He signals our spiritual GPS to re-route us.

Suspicion made me defensive and
less likely to trust.

I was so desperate to be accepted, I told my secrets and dreams to some people who would eventually betray me or compete with me. If I didn't value me, why should they? God often showed me the downfall of those relationships. I dismissed what I saw in them to be accepted. After my grandmother died, I tried to replace the comfort she'd given me by compromising myself, but only God could give me that comfort.

Remember, I was broken, and to be honest, some of the people I was attached to were just as broken as I was, but I couldn't see myself as the victim. I heard someone say, "You often attract what you are." Two dysfunctional people can never function well together. They constantly blame the other for the dysfunction in the relationship and accept it because it is their norm. Do you see yourself in this description?

There were genuine people who I tried to befriend. It didn't work because I allowed rotten relationships to contaminate the fruit-producing ones. I was always suspicious of women because many of them hurt me. My guardedness intimidated a lot of people who truly wanted to love me. Suspicion made me defensive and less likely to trust.

Whenever things started going well, I allowed them to crumble because I was too afraid they would end up like all my other relationships. To change this, I first had to form a covenant relationship with God. You can't be a true friend to anyone when you are not a friend to Him.

I would eat myself happy then be even more
depressed and guilty about it when I was done.

Wrong personal relationships weren't the only things I struggled with; food was my ultimate attachment. I wrestled in that area for a long time. Oh, how I loved food! It would not let me down or talk back. It comforted me. When I met my husband, I was one hundred eighty pounds and content. By the time I was at the height of my emotional downfall, a hundred and nine extra pounds crept on me. Fifty of them were gained during the honeymoon stage of courting.

You know how it is, you are so wrapped up in love, you forget about you. I didn't know comfortable eating would eventually turn into a battleground of depression. There were times I ate so much my stomach hurt. It was easy to gain a pound in a single seating. I remember passing by the mirror after I'd gotten out of the shower one day and was shocked at how I allowed myself to look. I sat on the side of the bed and cried my eyes out. I'd abused my body for so long, I barely recognized who I had become. How did I not notice my clothes no longer fit? I went from a size twelve to a size twenty, eating myself happy. I felt guilty and more depressed when I was done, but it was short-lived. I would eat again to feed the depression. I didn't recognize my own body.

There was a part of me that thought what I was going through was normal. Life weighed so heavy on me, I almost committed suicide. I got angry at God for allowing me to go through this pain, for not coming to my rescue. It was His fault. Why wouldn't He just save me? I decided to do it myself. Late one Saturday evening after I cried myself sick, I was in so much pain my heart couldn't take it anymore. The enemy kept whispering to me, "Why don't you end it all, no one cares," "Life would be better without you." I gathered myself off the bedroom floor and headed towards the kitchen because I believed him.

I was a grown woman stuck in childhood phases.

I'd made peace with the fact that it would all be over soon. I grabbed the sharpest knife I could find, went back to the bedroom, sat down and turned my wrist over. I can still feel the cold steel resting against my skin. Then, something brought me back to my senses. I cried out to God, "Help me!" dropped the knife, ran into the living room, crawled on my couch in the fetal position and began to cry even harder. I don't know if it was because I was mad God intervened or because a part of me really wanted to live. I was a grown woman stuck in different phases of my life. Shortly after, my husband came through the front door. He didn't speak or ask me what was wrong, he just laid over me and wept too. Someone else wanted me to survive.

I have come a long way since those dark hours. God saw my pain, but He didn't take pity on me. I needed all the letdowns and hardships so He could get the glory. It wasn't until I learned who I was in Christ that I began to understand, the relationship I was having with food was no good. Sometimes we have to experience the worst in our lives so God can show us the best.

Although I still have emotional scars, I forgave the things and people who put them there, even me. It was a long road to recovery. I shut myself off from the world. Unfortunately, I lost some people along the way as I transitioned, but if I tried to hold on to them, I could have permanently lost myself. I took inventory of my life, but we will get to it later.

It was time to prioritize my life and make
covenant relationships designed to propel me
into my destiny.

In the later part of 2014, I began to ask myself the hard questions. What role did you play in these failed relationships? What are you still holding on to? What do you need to let go of? Who do you need to let go of? I unplugged from everything that was draining Tamisha! The process was hard, but I needed to be free. I started with the most difficult component, my mind. I asked God to regulate my thoughts and shed light on the lies I had been believing. I started putting myself first. I began to see who was really in my corner when I began to focus on me. Some people can't build you up the way you've built them up. It was one of the hardest things to accept. If you look close enough, God always shows you the motives of those in your camp before He begins to elevate you. We must catch the revelation.

I was tired and needed energy and nourishment from the main source, the Power Source. It was time to prioritize my life and make covenant relationships designed to propel me into destiny. I prayed the powerful prayer I think all of us who are sick and tired of where we are pray, "Lord remove anything and anyone out of my life that is a hindrance to the things you have for me." I must admit, I was a bit surprised at who and what He removed. It is funny how life's hardest lessons thrust us into what God intended for us all along. Our mistakes should humble us. We must allow them to make us better, not bitter.

While God was dealing with me, there was no time to focus on anything but the vision He had for me. I came back to these pages to write more passionately about what God was still doing in my life. Writing this book was one of the tasks I put off because I allowed myself to become distracted. Once we begin to plug into our Source, then we can properly recharge. All we go through is not in vain, for the word says, "But as for you, you meant evil against me; but God meant it for good" (Genesis 50:20). I vowed to find the good in every bad situation and use it as a testimony to help others. Through all of this, I found self-love, but it came at a price, though it was one I did not mind paying.

I made God a priority and He embraced me like the prodigal son's father did him (Luke 15:11-32). What we go through is often a set up to get us to a place where we understand God is the only person who can fill the void in our lives. I had neglected our friendship and allowed imposters to come in and take His place. With Him as my focus, I no longer had to depend on fake friends, bad relationships or food. I still have a love affair with food, but we have come to an understanding. It no longer reigns over my life. I am back into the arms of the One I strayed from, He loved me right where I was.

God shows us true love so we can identify those who don't love us the way we should be loved. I wish I could say it will happen overnight, but I can say, in time wounds do heal. If we cover them up, the process is prolonged. Forgive, I can't stress this enough. It is simple to say, but so hard to do. One thing that kept me from moving on from broken relationships was my unwillingness to forgive. I thought I had, but as soon as something happened again, or I would be in their presence, it took me back to the place of wounding. I suppressed my feelings about the situation, separated myself from the people, and never properly healed. When God showed me I had not forgiven, I made a conscious effort to fix it. Didn't God forgive us after we broke His heart? Forgiveness does not excuse the person's behavior, but it does free you from it. If I wanted to be free, I had to forgive. I started by forgiving myself for giving people permission to use and violate me. I forgave myself for not putting God first.

Start freeing yourself by forgiving. Stop living in past hurts or being a victim to people who have already moved on with their lives. John 8:36 declares, "Who the Son has set free is free indeed." Take back your Freedom!

Deliverance Prayer

Lord, I come to You as humbly as I know how to ask Your forgiveness for attaching myself to things You didn't put in my life. Help me to identify all attachments which will not edify Your Kingdom. Give me the strength to walk away from them and boldly stand beside You as You continue to guide me. Help me to understand, man's rejection is Your protection and Your acceptance is all I need. I am your beloved and your love for me is strong. It can't be severed by the opinions or thoughts of those who once rejected me. Help me to love them unconditionally. I know when they reject me, they are also rejecting You. Give me the strength to continue to walk in confidence and grace. Amen

Exercise 4

1. What has caused defeat in your life?

_____

_____

_____

_____

_____

_____

2. What past relationships are you allowing to hold you back from becoming the person you are destined to be?

_____

_____

_____

_____

_____

_____

3. What do you need to forgive yourself for?

_____

_____

_____

_____

_____

_____

4. Who do you need to FORGIVE?

_____

_____

_____

_____

_____

5. What steps will you take to make God your priority?

_____

_____

_____

_____

_____

Chapter Five

SPIRIT OF REJECTION

The door of rejection stayed open in my life. I always loved hard and the harder I loved, the easier I made it for others to take advantage of me. My harsh reality? I loved the wrong people. The struggle with rejection made me want to give more than I had to offer. As a little girl, I always tried to gain my mother's acceptance, anything for her approval. I thought the more I did for her, the more she would love me. Even my best was not good enough. Her rejection caused psychological issues that haunted me as an adult. All I wanted was to feel her love.

A mother is her daughter's first teacher. Although I had some wonderful women in my life, they couldn't give me the love and affection I desired from the one in whose womb I spent nine months. The mother-daughter division has long-lasting effects. It explains why some women have problems with others. Maybe because they have the same characteristics as their mothers. It is all too common today.

The spirit of rejection is like any other spirit, it is ancient, traveling from generation to generation. Look at the relationship between your mother and her mother, or even the generation before. What similarities do you see? We need to confront existing issues, but not without God. Remember, we must dig up the root before we can heal. If we don't, we only pass the seed down to our future daughters. They pass them down to their children.

When a young girl is properly loved by her mother, there is no need to go looking for love in things and people who diminish her value. It is important for mothers to love their daughters in a way that is essential to their development. When they don't, subconsciously that young girl takes on the characteristics and habits of her mother. It manifests as a lack of self-esteem and has a lasting effect on all her relationships, including marriage.

I wasn't taught how to love by my mother. This not only effected some relationships I had with women; it deeply affected the relationship I had with my husband. My mother was not to blame for the problems we had, but the seed of rejection she'd planted kept producing fruit. At the time, I hadn't yet found it.

I was madly in love with my husband from the first day I saw him. He gave me something I hadn't received since Ms. Cat, unconditional love. I treasured the idea of someone loving me as much as he did. It had been a long time since I felt that. My grandmother had been dead at least seven years by then.

Some marriages are destroyed because the wife has been rejected by her mother and it affects the way she handles relationships. A good man comes along but because she has been mentally tormented by a lack of motherly love, she doesn't know how to accept his affection. She sabotages a great relationship. In extreme cases, she gets into abusive relationships because she feels if her own mother can't love her, she must be undeserving.

The spirit of rejection lingers. It took some time for me to realize it was a spirit. If you don't recognize what you are dealing with, you can't defeat it. I was operating from the carnal mind; my spiritual mind had not yet matured. The spirit became so familiar, I thought I needed to embrace it and those who imposed it on me by trying to love them even more. I couldn't love the rejection away. I'd exhausted myself with people-pleasing, thinking it was normal behavior. I thought it was wrong to put myself first. Some of us do anything for people to receive us, which is why many in the body of Christ compromise. We're dependent on people and believe it's only through them we can accomplish what God has given us to do.

I believed the amount of love I got was based on how much I did for people. If you did more, they would love you more. I just couldn't understand why people were not reciprocating. My perspective was clouded by my need to be needed. I allowed myself to be tormented by the feelings of rejection for so long, I thought it was normal behavior. When my husband came along, I didn't know how to handle his unconditional love.

The spirit of rejection plays with your mind and attacks your self-esteem. You feel worthless, and when you are no longer connected to the only person you think can fill the void, you believe the enemy's lies and become defeated. That's why it's imperative we get to know God. I had to get to a place where I desired Him more than being accepted. I strongly believe there are dynamic ministries waiting to be birthed, but they are held up by the spirit of rejection. We want more of man than we do of God, and compromise His ability to use us because our faith is in those we want to esteem us.

I was tired of being rejected and hurt. My heart grew hard, my ways even harder, angry, bitter, determined not to allow people to hurt me again. I secretly held grudges against those who rejected me. I was suspicious of everyone, and if I thought they were getting close to me, I was ready to strike without reservation. I was deteriorating from the inside out because of bitterness and no longer recognized myself, forever paranoid of people and their motives pertaining to me. After you've been rejected for as long as I had, you tend to become afraid. In my eyes, everybody wanted something.

My paranoia killed some of my relationships. They got backlash because of what someone else did. I grew impatient with people and cut them out of my life. As the cliché says, I dropped you like a bad habit and wouldn't look back. The fact that I cut people out of my life was not the problem, it was the mean grudge I held inside my heart. It was a wall that blocked many of my blessings. The dangerous thing about you being the victim of my grudges is that you didn't know it. I would speak kindly, but if thoughts could kill, you would be dead instantly. The smile on my face was as fake as I felt. However, that was my little secret.

I was tired. I'd finally come to a point where I was asking myself the hard questions. Why are you so needy? Why do you feel you need man more than God? Why are you still trying to prove yourself? If I wanted to be free of rejection and those who caused it, I had to dig deep for these answers. That was a scary time. I was consumed with anger and hurt. The angrier I got, the harder my heart became towards those who hurt me. Imagine how ugly my heart was as I carried those feelings. It would be years before I was free of the pain or have the capacity to let go of the ones who caused it. Some took longer than others, but I eventually did. Talk about a burden being lifted. Whew!

Once my eyes were open, I could see how God must have felt when I spent so much time rejecting Him. I'd abandoned Him while searching for acceptance from the same people that could not produce fruit in my life. I looked for answers from those who had none. I shared the visions God had given me with them but did not give back to the One who had given those visions to me. I never considered God's feelings. I am thankful He never gave up on me.

Satan attacks us at our most vulnerable moments. The attack is so sudden you have no time to react. Transitioning from that mindset was hard, but I grew through it. I came out of the season solely dependent on God, praising Him for those who left me, those who rejected me, those who counted me out. I even praised Him for allowing it to happen. It was for my good. My prayer life grew, my praise grew, my worship grew, and so did my independence. I was finally becoming the person God knew I could become. I was growing into God-confidence.

While I was going through this, my husband told me of a dream he had about me. It was more confirmation I was coming out of that dark place and would be victorious. In the dream, a King Cobra was attacking me. It struck multiple times, but the strikes did not affect me. It made me think of the scripture in Acts 28:3-5. "Paul gathered a pile of brushwood and, as he put it on the fire, a viper, driven out by the heat, fastened itself on his hand. When the islanders saw the snake hanging from his hand, they said to each other, "This man must be a murderer; for though he escaped from the sea, the goddess Justice has not allowed him to live." But Paul shook the snake off into the fire and suffered no ill effects." As Paul put wood on the fire, the viper came from amongst the heat and struck Paul's hand. A viper is amongst one of the most dangerous snakes and its bite can be deadly, but much like Paul, in the dream, I too was unaffected.

When the snake could not take me down with its bite, it spat venom in my eyes. The eyes are vulnerable. Interrupted sight causes blurred vision. Blurred vision hinders destiny. Since the serpent could not attack my body, he was trying to make me blind. It was imperative I keep my eyes on this journey. No matter what the enemy sent my way, I would remain focused.

A King Cobra's venom is powerful. The toxins affect the victim's central nervous system, resulting in severe pain, blurred vision, vertigo, drowsiness, and eventually paralysis. If the envenomation is serious, it progresses to cardiovascular collapse, and the victim falls into a coma. Death soon follows due to respiratory failure.[2] This is how the enemy tries to hinder us in the spirit. He uses everything in his power to harm us when we begin to walk with God. As the venom travels through our spiritual nervous system, its goal is to break us down until our vision is the last to be affected. If you don't let him take your eyes of God, you may be wounded, but you won't be defeated.

After God gave me the revelation of the dream, I took inventory of my life and was immediately strengthened. I thought about all the strikes of rejection I received and how each dose of venom only made me stronger. I became immune to the poison. I was no longer affected by the fear of rejection. The stronghold of people-pleasing was no more. As I embraced God, I depended less on people. The will of God became the center of my life, it outweighed the spirit of rejection the enemy had planted. God protected me.

Once you conquer the spirit of rejection, you will be able to detect it as soon as it is present. You won't let offense set in and you can pray for the person the enemy used against you. The things which caused great pain will no longer affect you. Rejection is one of the hardest spirits to overcome. It plays on the mind and because you may not understand what you are fighting, you feel defenseless.

If you suffer from the spirit of rejection, it will show up in every area in your life – your job, friendships, family relationships, and even the church. People who have been rejected are some of the most sensitive, which is why they are amongst powerful people in the kingdom of God. They have a gift the enemy does not want them to discover. Sensitivity in the spirit leads the Believer to a new dimension in Christ. God is a healer and He wants to deliver you.

Even though my battle was long and hard, God brought me out. There are times when the enemy still tries to attack me with the spirit of rejection, but because I now know what weapons he uses, I don't rest there. Once you conquer the spirt, you can handle the person who displays it. Prayer is your best defense.

You may feel no one is there for you. Maybe you were neglected as a child, rejected by your friends, family or even your spouse. Guess what? God will use it, sometimes to mold you into the person He's designed you to be. Your testimony will be... GOD DID IT!

Deliverance Prayer

Heavenly Father, You are our protector. You love us so much you want what's best for our lives. Please give us the strength to unconditionally love those who reject us. Help us to understand, when You tell us no, it is only for our good. Heal the bitterness toward those who despitefully use us. Help us to realize it is Your love which validates and confirms who You have called us to be. Let us be content with who we are in You, so much we are confident and made strong through this season. Fill any void that needs to be filled to get us to a place of complete dependence on You. Give us an unprecedented peace surpassing our understanding. Help us to rely, not on our emotions, but on Your love to completely shield us.
Amen

Exercise 5

What experiences of rejection have left scars in your life? Write them down, face your rejection and be heal from it.

1._____

_____

_____

_____

_____

_____

2._____

_____

_____

_____

_____

3._____

_____

_____

_____

_____

_____

4._____

_____

_____

_____

_____

_____

5._____

_____

_____

_____

_____

Chapter Six

SILENCE AS A WEAPON

As a child, I remember my grandmother on the porch talking with her peers. They often used the phrase "their mouth would be the death of them," referring to someone who liked to gossip. I never forgot those words. Later, they would come back to haunt me. Even at that age, I had big visions, and my mouth was the key indicator of how much I dreamed. I talked to anyone who listened. As I think of those conversations, my grandmother and her friends were on to something I was just too young to understand. It was an indirect warning to be careful with my mouth. I became painfully aware as an adult.

My mouth was also the death of a lot of my dreams. Some never happened and others were stolen and developed by others. Sometimes we want to share what God is doing in our lives with the world. Our genuine happiness for others makes us naively think they will show us the same enthusiasm. It took many years and plenty of betrayals to recognize, this. I can't blame it all on Satan or others though, I sabotaged myself. I gave my dreams away and had the audacity to get mad about it.

As I think of lost dreams, Sarah and Hagar come to mind (Galatians 4:21-31). Sarah was Abraham's wife and Hagar was

Sarah's servant. God promised Abraham many descendants would come from his loins. However, ten years after the promise, Sarah is still barren, and they are both weary of waiting. Instead of believing God and being patient, Sarah gave Hagar to Abraham, in accordance with the customs of those days, so Sarah could have a child through her (Genesis 16:2). Hagar conceived, and Sarah despised her. She dealt with her harshly, causing Hagar to flee to the desert to escape her mistress' resentment. That was me, some time ago, too impatient to wait on the Lord to manifest my visions. Unlike Sarah, I did it unknowingly. I prematurely spoke about them and someone I trusted brought them to life. Like Sarah, I had a lot of resentment.

In our impatience, we try to help God and end up waiting even longer for our dreams to manifest. Ultimately, what God has for us is ours, but our willingness to continue to veer off course will determine if we ever see it materialize. If you keep reading Abraham and Sarah's story, the angel relayed the same promise, "I will surely multiply your offspring so that they cannot be numbered for multitude" (Genesis 16:10). Not only did he repeat the promise, he also told them what sex the baby would be, his name and character (Genesis 16:11-12).

God confirms His promises to us. Sarah eventually saw hers but look at all that transpired because she did not trust God. In my case, impatience came in the form of my big mouth and my ability to keep it running. I had to learn to shut it. God took me into complete isolation. There was no one to talk to and in the silence, I began to hear His voice more clearly. He taught me to depend on Him, not my own understanding. I was no longer led by my emotions. Although heartache and pain brought me to this encounter, it was all in His plan. Everything made perfect sense.

There were times when all I wanted to do was talk to someone, but no one was available, well at least not how I expected them to be. As God dealt with me, I no longer needed to be socially accepted. One of my ministry friends called this time the incubation period and it sure felt like it. I needed prayer, compassion, and love, instead, I got backlash, drama, and accusations. This was a lonely walk. Is this how Jesus felt during His journey? It seems I dealt with more spiritual attacks while in the will of God than I did in the world. It's one reason many people don't see His fullness because the pressure is too much to handle.

Once I stopped depending on people for answers, God said, "I will use this silence to keep you focused." I had been going in the wrong direction, trying to help others who knew it but were too selfish to tell me because they were benefiting. God moved them out of the way, and I gave Him my undivided attention. He called me to a deeper more intimate relationship with Him. I no longer resisted. My desire was to be alone with Him as much as He sought to spend time with me. The Lord could do a better job of handling my battles. It was time for me to rest. He used my former leader to confirm this by encouraging me with Psalm 37, highly emphasizing the words, commit, delight, rest, and trust. As I applied those words to my life, it became more God-centered.

The silence thing was not feeling so good. There was no one to blame, no one to point fingers at, just me. God shed light on some of my hidden insecurities and the only way He could do that was in the dark. With all my outward confidence, inner confidence was nowhere to be found. God exposed me to me. I had to face my biggest fears. As I got closer to my core issues I began to appreciate being in the dark. It was less intimidating. God's light on my insecurities brought deliverance. I embraced what was happening.

Webster describes silence as, "a situation, state, or period of time in which people do not talk." It would be farfetched for me to say I no longer talked to people. I still talked, just not about the details of this journey God and I were on. I had been idolizing people, making them mini gods, when God was the only one with the answers to free me from bondage. I needed to be free from my internal battles. I pleaded with God to soothe the pain and rush the process. The more I begged for it to be over, the greater the pressure got. Every issue came to the surface as if the last thirty years were flashing before my eyes at rapid speed.

I'd lost myself, and this reintroduction to Tamisha was very uncomfortable because the wilderness had become my new normal. The more God pushed me toward destiny, the more I wanted to stay there. It is funny how we can be in the midst of a mess for so long our dysfunction feels functional. I was a dysfunction addict if there is such a thing. I came close to self-destructing. I've heard, the definition of insanity is doing the same thing over and over again expecting a different result. I was on the verge of insanity because I was afraid. It was impossible to motivate myself to do even things that would help me. I'm not sure if I was more afraid of being unsuccessful or if it was the thought of how much my life would change.

As every stronghold was exposed, there was an urgency to address it. God turned every stone over and exposed what was under it. While my younger self wrestled with the woman I was becoming, I unpacked years of baggage and God made sure I emptied it all. He wants pure hearts to do His mighty works, so He purges those He's handpicked to get them ready, just like Jesus did with His disciples (Matthew 4:18-22). I needed to be cleansed from everything that would make me less effective. You learn a lot of things about yourself when you accept responsibility. I wish I'd made a conscious decision to do so a long time ago.

My biggest asset to others is my ability to motivate them. I've helped countless people reach their goals, but I couldn't reach mine. Part of me hoped someone would motivate me and push me to greatness. After all, I joined forces with them to make sure their ventures happened. I help you, you help me, right? The hard truth was, I never had true confidence in my ability to become who God purposed me to be. I hid behind working for others, secretly believing it was the only way I would get closer to my dreams. This went on for a few years. How unfortunate I didn't know my strength or value.

In the silence came God's wisdom. I grew in that space. I'm thankful He did not give up on me, even when I wasn't acknowledging Him. My prayer life grew, my praise increased, I worshiped more, and I became more dependent on God. Even though I lost a few people on the journey, this brought me to a closer relationship with God. My silence killed the enemy's plans. I could see what he was trying to do in my life. In what was a dark time, much light shined also. You may be in that place now. If you are, allow it to become your weapon. In those times His still small voice speaks volumes.

Deliverance Prayer

Lord, I don't understand this season of my life, but I do know You are in control. Help me to trust you in the dark. Allow me to lean, not on my own understanding, but to acknowledge Your hands as You guide me from the dark to Your light. As I walk in this season of silence, I give You all the things that will not benefit my life. If this journey gets darker help me to know Your light will always shine through as a reminder of who You are and how You will continue to keep me in perfect peace. Comfort me and assure me You are with me. Amen!

Exercise 6

During my time of silence, God revealed areas in my life that lacked proper spiritual nutrition. Although it was challenging, I was able through the grace of God to face and conquer difficult areas. Do you feel like God is calling you to a place of stillness? If so, what are some areas in your life that need His light? It is time to identify them. Take inventory of those things and ask God to help you.

1._____

_____

_____

_____

_____

_____

2._____

_____

_____

_____

_____

_____

3._____

_____

_____

_____

_____

_____

4._____

_____

_____

_____

_____

_____

5._____

_____

_____

_____

_____

_____

Chapter Seven

FORGIVENESS

God started to deal with me about some people and situations I had buried so deep it was almost as if they never occurred. Their residue lingered and affected me greatly. One afternoon, in a meeting with the Bishop of my church, he told me a story of a young man and his will to forgive. He explained how he had forgiven his mother for doing something heinous to him. At first, I thought it was way off subject, but it was a message from God for me; a well overdue divine appointment. He got me thinking about the need to truly forgive. I'd entered the Bishop's office in bondage and walked out feeling free.

This conversation was only confirmation of what God had been tugging on my heart about for weeks. During my season of silence, forgiveness was amongst the many things I needed to do. I had to forgive to properly heal. We constantly hear forgiveness is not about the person who hurt us, it is about us. That is one of the truest statements I've ever heard. When we forgive, we release people from taking up space in our lives and make room for the blessings that were held up by our unwillingness to forgive. It took me almost two decades to grasp this. Forgiveness is powerful.

How could I be a Christian, love the Lord, do all the things I believed were necessary to meet Him one day, and still be holding on to unforgiveness? To be honest, I didn't know. It explained some of the bitterness I had been carrying secretly. For a long time, I allowed unresolved issues and hurt to remain in my heart. When we allow burdens to lay dormant, they eventually awaken a beast (unforgiveness) that's not easily tamed.

Don't ignore issues from broken relationships. It is dangerous to have an out of sight out of mind mentality. Most of the time we would rather not see the person again. When we don't address past hurts, those who have hurt us can't redeem themselves. People move on, sometimes never knowing what they've done to offend us. In many cases, it wasn't even intentional.

Many of my bad experiences remained unresolved after the people who caused them were no longer in my life. It is dangerous to cover up old wounds, they become infected. Once we encounter the person again, we are suspicious of their motives and secretly hold what they've done over their heads. We convince ourselves we're guarding our hearts. In reality, we have not properly healed. The residue of unforgiveness festers.

Even if you do form a relationship with the person, it will never last. Depending on the severity of the hurt, no matter what they do, you can't truly trust them. You are constantly reminded of what they once did to you. I'm not saying don't be mindful when dealing with that person, what I am saying is, don't let it control your emotions. Be led by the Holy Spirit when dealing with such people. Some individuals are cruel. Stay away from them, but to have peace, you must forgive. Their issues may be deeper than you know. Keep your peace even if they don't say sorry. Sometimes it's better if they don't apologize at all.

We tend to look at things according to our past experiences and not reality. After someone hurts us intentionally, they may change but because we never forgave them, we can't see it. We put up a wall that keeps us bound. The person has moved on and we are still waiting for an apology when they've already forgotten about what they have done.

Unforgiveness is a spirit, a poison that will stunt spiritual growth if undetected. It causes bitterness and resentment and eats away at us spiritually and mentally. It is amongst the most popular tools the enemy uses to keep God's people from their destinies. Like cancer, the longer it goes undetected, the faster it spreads until it fully consumes us. This may seem farfetched to some, but this spirit leads to more physical problems like sickness and diseases. It opens us to curses. We give them room to attach themselves to our offspring and spread to future generations. Don't give this spirit room in your heart.

When God had me go through my box labeled, unforgiveness, He touched on my relationship with my husband. Let me talk to some of my married women. This may be a sensitive subject, but if you can digest it, I promise it will start your healing progress. I married at a young age, still broken, fragile and immature. I wanted to fill a void only God could fill. My husband had the same struggle too. I have often heard women say, "He completes me." News flash, marriage will not solve your problems and it will not complete you! Don't believe the hype. You must seek to be whole before you say I do.

I was not emotionally healthy when I got married. The abandoned, broken and neglected little girl inside me was incapable of loving anyone, including myself. I had no business entertaining the thought of marriage let alone following through with the commitment. What did I know, at twenty-one, about a commitment and before God at that? I hadn't even begun to live.

When we are not ready to enter matrimony, we do more damage than good to ourselves and our spouses. The divorce rate in the Christian community is higher than any other organized religion. Marriage relationships take time to grow, but often we are more excited about the fairy tale wedding than the actual journey. Do you mind if I get transparent? My marriage was painfully hard during our earlier years. I cried many nights because the twelve-year-old girl whose hurts were never dealt with, the one who needed to be loved properly, was very much alive, and she kept coming to the surface. The enemy used her against me in my marriage. He also used others to remind me of the pain.

I resented my husband. I wanted him to protect me from the pain and the people who inflicted it. I made Him my god and when he could not perform the duties only God could, I resented him more. We couldn't love each other the way we both needed to be loved. I won't go into specific details because we don't live there anymore, but I will tell you, we had given up on us. There were unsigned divorce papers to prove it, yet we survived infidelity, rumors, vicious lies, hate, and personal attacks.

He was supposed to leave his family and cleave to his wife. They should no longer be first in his life. He was my husband. I wanted God to personally hold him accountable for disrupting the order of our house. He was the head. He should hurt as badly as I hurt. I needed to forgive him, but situations kept presenting themselves. When he missed opportunities to defend me those old emotions rose up again and we would be back to square one. I could not stay away from the past long enough to deal with the real issues. Rejection caused havoc in this area of my life. There were still weeds in that part of my garden.

If you keep bringing up the past, it's a sign you're still wrestling with unforgiveness. Do you become angry when you talk about previous experiences? This too is a residue of unforgiveness. Only after I'd dealt with those childhood issues was I able to forgive my husband. No, he did not apologize for what happened, nor did he acknowledge his wrongdoing at the time. Whether he was going to or not, I knew my relationship with God was more important than the burden I was carrying.

I wanted my marriage to work. We had been divided for so long it felt normal. I wanted the pain to end and for us to become one flesh. I decided to stop fighting my husband and started fighting the enemy with spiritual weapons instead. No longer was I trying to fix things with my wearied flesh. I covered our marriage in prayer and bound things which caused the division in our relationship. The more I chose to forgive my husband, the more the enemy attacked our union, but God said, "Keep fighting, keep forgiving!" It was hard work, and it kept me on my knees. I went to God about myself instead of going to Him about my husband. I'd walked around with such bitterness in my heart toward him. I was also part of the problem. My issues started even before I met him.

Here came the hard part. I had to first take care of the twelve-year-old girl who had followed me into adulthood. I needed to forgive her for tormenting me with the pains of my past. I also had to forgive myself for allowing others to define me. It was time to take responsibility for all the things I allowed to happen.

I was no longer a prisoner of rejection. I took back the power I had given away. It was not my husband's fault I was mistreated as a child. It was not my fault I was not given the life the average child received. It would be my fault if I continued to allow it to define the woman God was trying to set free. Once I did that, my marriage began to heal. It was rough at first, but we worked through it.

Since then, every day God shows me areas where He has matured us. Instead of focusing on the past, we keep our eyes on God and how He is molding us now. My husband still gets on my nerves at times and I know I get on his, but we love each other dearly. If I could give you ladies any marital advice it would be to keep family out of your business and pray for your spouse.

During this process God taught me how to be a wife, well at least the wife He wanted for the husband He had given me. He instructed me to stop nagging. Nagging only makes your spouse rebel and pushes them further away. God was the only one who could change my husband. We also learned to submit. Submission does not mean being a slave, it means you respect and honor the union. This is often hard to do, especially when you are going through hard times in your marriage. When you submit in the worst situations, God moves mightily.

Let me touch on adultery. I am not condemning anyone; I want us to be free! Our spouses know what we are doing. Don't think God has not shown them. A moment of pleasure is not worth God's wrath. Get to the root of the issue. Every time we step outside our marriage, we are creating strongholds only God can free us from. When I was in the stronghold of adultery, it was not enjoyable. My mind was clouded by a false sense of reality. I thought running from my problems to another man would make things better. It never does, in fact, it makes things worse.

When we get to this place in our marriage, the problem is bigger than we think. Unforgiveness and the resentment it creates causes bad decisions. My prayer is that none of you reading this have to deal with adultery, but if by chance you have or are dealing with it now, there is still hope. God is a restorer of marriages. He restored mine. I am glad my husband and I chose to stand when the enemy wanted us to fold. We're not a perfect couple, but we are perfect for one another.

Your spouse may not be who we think they should be, but you married them. Ask God to help them become who He wants them to be. Get rid of unforgiveness. Let God fix your marriage. Release the hurt and support your spouse. They need you. The worst thing they can experience is being beaten up by the world, then coming home to the same treatment from you. If you are angry with them, call right now and apologize. Tell them you love them.

When unforgiveness stays in our hearts, we give the enemy permission to rob us of our blessings, and our joy. The unforgiveness in my heart got in through the door of rejection. I had to take inventory of everyone I had not forgiven and address the person or the hurt. As I sought God for wisdom, He gave me revelation to discern if the person caused the pain or if it was just my perception. In some situations where I claimed to be the victim, I had to apologize to the actual victims. It was an awakening. I confronted my demons. In some cases, the demon I confronted was me. It takes God's help to do that kind of work. It was extremely painful because I was finally facing my truth.

As crazy as it seems, the pain brought about the biggest breakthroughs. All things serve a purpose, even our pain. Pain will shift you to greater you if you allow it. As God continued to work in me, one of my requests was that He remove images of events that negatively affected me. I wanted to forget them. "For I will be merciful to their unrighteousness, and their sins and their iniquities will I remember no more" (Hebrews 8:12). This scripture ministered to me. If God could be merciful to me after I hurt Him and not only forgive me but also forget my sins and transgressions, He gave me the capacity to do the same. I let Him lead me in all things so I would not repeat painful actions.

Unforgiveness prevents God from forgiving our sins and I had a lot I needed Him to forgive. It would have been a travesty if I died still angry with those who trespassed against me. I thank God for being patient with me during trying moments. As I forgave, He released His best for me. Satan does not want us to forgive because he knows once we do, our lives will be immediately transformed. We were created to love one another.

We tend to only love on the surface. Unconditional love is so much more. It's the ability and the willingness to love someone even when they don't love you. The word of God says, "love covers a multitude of sins" (1 Peter 4:8). I now fully understand this scripture. God's love saved me and gave me strength to compassionately and unconditionally love the people who used and hurt me. He loved me first and I choose to love the way He does.

Allow God to heal your wounds. Tell Him all about them. This journey won't be easy, but if you forgive, it will be life changing. You won't be able to do it in your own strength. Let God transform you. Are you ready? Let's pray!

Deliverance Prayer

Father God, we come to You asking first that You forgive us our debts, as we forgive those who trespass against us. Free us from the pain that has buried us and give us strength to walk through every painful situation that has hindered us and stunted our growth. Help us to form a more intimate relationship with You so we will no longer accept relationships that are not for us. You said whom the Son has set free is free indeed. We accept the freedom only You can give. We come together (all who are reading this) and pray this prayer in Your name, the marvelous matchless name of Jesus Christ. Amen!

"For if you forgive men when they sin against you, your heavenly Father will also forgive you. But if you do not forgive men their sins, your Father will not forgive your sins."
Colossians 3:13 NIV

Exercise 7

There is power in forgiveness. What or who are you unwilling to forgive? Search deep within yourself and release that situation or person. You have held it in for too long, it is time to release it. Before you move on to the next chapter, write it down and give it to God. He is waiting on you.

1._____

_____

_____

_____

_____

_____

2._____

_____

_____

_____

_____

3._____

_____

_____

_____

_____

_____

4._____

_____

_____

_____

_____

_____

5._____

_____

_____

_____

_____

_____

.

Chapter Eight

DEAD WEIGHT

August 21, 2014 is a day I will never forget. It was the day my burdens began to fall off. I wrestled with God, like Jacob. His instructions were specific and strategic. They left no room for misunderstanding, yet we tussled a good while (it took three attempts) before I finally gave up. He explained that blessings would not flow to my life until I fully surrendered. I knew I was a hot mess and God did too. With every tug, He released strongholds - pain, depression, anger, bitterness, fear, doubt, and oppression. I too was left with a limp (Genesis 32:22-32). My favorite prayer was, "God, I want to look in the mirror and see a new person." He answered my prayer, but I had to do the work.

In the book of Exodus, the children of Israel spent many years in the wilderness because they complained, murmured and doubted God. I spent four years in my wilderness, walking in circles just like the Israelites. It was lonely, there was no pity party, no wiping of my tears, just silence from God. I was drained circling the wilderness. The more I complained, the harder it got. I walked in circles for so long, the trails became bloodstained. I'd worn out the soles of my shoes and ripped open the bottoms of my feet. If my tears wouldn't move God, I wanted to know what would.

True motives and intentions reveal themselves when we are under pressure. Every corner of my wilderness was labeled - rejection, unhealthy attachments, unforgiveness, fear, and shame. Gardens of insecurities and unresolved issues were planted there. I had to uproot every one of them before I could get to my promise land. I was determined to battle what had been battling my mind. My fight was no longer with God, it was for God. There were times when I grew weary, but He strengthened me.

The blessing is understanding the wilderness is a season for your breakthrough. It is a time when your heart is tested. How you spend your time there determines the magnitude of your breakthrough. It became clear it was my training ground. I no longer saw my issues as burdens, they were assignments. God taught me to successfully study the root of my pain and properly dig it up. I hope I'm not making this sound easy. It was a struggle before I matured enough to realize the journey was good for me. Once I figured out the formula, it was easier to past my tests. Honey, the weight of my issues began to fall off me like melted butter on a hot knife, but I was not in the clear yet. I had to retake tests multiple times because I kept trying to cheat my way out. There are no short cuts to destiny. He trained me in the dark so I would appreciate the light.

I thought I could out slick God, but it wasn't easy. The tests were not on Scantron paper, filled in with a pencil. The answers were in my heart and He was the gatekeeper. He held the key. When I got tired of cheating, I asked Him for the wisdom, patience and instructions needed to pass the test. Before long, I started trusting Him to do the things fathers do, like protect. I never had a father figure in my life. My natural father wasn't around until I was an adult. I met my heavenly Father in the wilderness and learned four valuable lessons there.

The wilderness protects us. It prevents us from going deeper into despair while God gets our attention. While pursuing my real estate career, I believed I was in the safe zone. How could this not be God's will? He could have easily elevated me, but He knew I was not ready for that kind of success. I would make a lot of money, but I was about to miss out on Him. Sometimes we don't realize we are in danger. Only God's will provides protection.

When we step outside it, we are fair game for the enemy.

I was chasing success, but my life was not aligned with God's will. The wilderness came shortly after. My bitter ways and impure motives would have bought me a one-way ticket to destruction. I didn't need money and power. They would hurt me or probably give me the opportunity to hurt others. I was not an angry person, nor have I ever set out to deliberately hurt people, but I did have a point to prove. I can admit, a part of me wanted to succeed to boast in the face of my enemies.

My eyes were set on my dream house, car, flourishing business and the money which would follow. I had big plans but was too ignorant to know God's plan. I went to church and paid my tithes, but our relationship was not solid. At the time, I couldn't understand why He allowed me to get so close to victory then snatched it from my reach.

I know many people who became successful trying to prove a point. I don't know if they are happy, what I do know is, I want to be whole before God elevates me, in fact, I prayed for it. I would have been victorious in man's eyes, and more broken and damaged in God's. He shielded me from self-exaltation. God's blessing is rich and adds no sorrow (Proverbs 10:22). I am glad He sees further than we do. I now look forward to my future.

God provides in the wilderness. Some think provision means financial gain and that's the only way to be blessed. God's provision is greater than material things. He gives peace of mind. My whole world fell apart in the wilderness season. You name it, it happened to me. It was as if the enemy gathered all his minions, grabbed their biggest weapons and launched them directly at me. There was no room to catch my breath. I felt like a tornado had swept up our house and thrown it across the country, leaving us naked and unprotected, but God provided. I had all the tools needed to keep me sane in the wilderness. He was all my husband and I needed.

Sometimes in our pursuit of happiness, we accumulate things God doesn't value. He drained every resource I had for help. He even made sure my husband couldn't be my back up. I had put too much hope in him. This was one of the tests I repeatedly failed. I blamed Him for what happened. I was laughed at, had fingers pointed at me, and He kept saying, you are walking in the right direction. His instructions were, keep moving your feet.

It took a while to accept that God alone was my provider – my Jehovah Jireh (Genesis 22:14). He delights in taking care of us. I no longer take it personally when people fail me. I see it as an opportunity to seek God and His guidance.

The wilderness prepares us for our God-given assignments. We are born to carry out His commission. Along the way, we may get off track. For those who have fallen off course, the wilderness realigns us to purpose, to finish what God started. If I had not gone through trials and tribulations, I could not minister about the goodness of God, or be able to help others become free. Strong foundations are built in the wilderness.

We miss the beauty of our journey because we don't value the process. Yes, it gets hard, but you must hold out to see what the end will be. Every great man and woman in the Bible had major obstacles and setbacks. Our setbacks are the most important parts of preparation. There were times I thought God was making a fool of me. I'm listening for His voice and He wants to make me look stupid? Really? Of course, this made me furious. It felt like He was playing games. Every time I thought I was being pushed further away from what God had for me, I was being better prepared for what I would face in the future. Expect your endurance to be tested.

To whom much is given, much is required (Luke 12:48). I know you are wondering why He doesn't just tell us all the things we need to do to get to the end of the process. I often pleaded with Him. When there is a calling on your life, God has to cover all bases. He makes sure you can handle the responsibility. Jeremiah 12:5 says, "If thou hast run with the footmen, and they have wearied thee, then how canst thou contend with horses?" This scripture is so profound. If we can't handle the small setbacks in our lives, how can we handle the larger ones? The higher God takes us, the bigger the challenges we face. God is less concerned about how long our process takes, and more about how well we are being prepared. Enjoy the small victories, the big ones are coming. The word of God says, "It is good for me that I have been afflicted; that I might learn thy statutes" (Psalms 119:71).

Lastly, the wilderness produces fruit. Like well plowed, fertilized soil, your wilderness produces a fresh harvest. Before the wilderness, I thought I had it all together - for the life I was trying to build, perhaps I did. God had other plans. We can't even begin to fathom what He has for us. He must train you to go where He leads. Your old ways and habits won't work. The wilderness produces character and births a brand-new individual.

Some linger in the wilderness longer than others, but that too is alright. Everyone's destiny is different, and some require just a little bit more refining. After all the tests are completed, God begins to reposition you to receive the harvest He was preparing for you all along. You are meant to die (to self) in the wilderness so you can be birthed. It sounds strange doesn't it; an oxymoron? How does one die and then live again? I'm not talking about physical death, but a spiritual one. You must die to everything which would rob you from the future God has for you. He will revive you with His purpose. Old thoughts, patterns, habits, even the old way of life, are no longer welcome.

After leaving my wilderness, God placed a new song in my heart. The path He had for me was no longer hidden. He began to bless me unexpectedly in different areas of my life. I could handle the gifts He gave. The harvest was evident. Often, we think God's blessings are always supposed to come gift wrapped with pretty bows. The wilderness is a place of transition before your breakthrough. If you are there now, or if you are headed there, breathe. It is not a place to be feared. The biggest blessings come after our most uncomfortable seasons. Delight yourself, commit and rest in the Lord. He led you to the wilderness to help you, not to harm you. What time is it? It's praying time, let's pray.

Deliverance Prayer

Heavenly Father, I come to You as humble as I know how. I seek your hand to cover me while I am in the wilderness. Help me to release all control and relinquish my whole heart to You. Help me to understand Your will for my life. Let me be at peace while I am in this place of transition. Give me a willingness to face the areas that need to be dealt with and give me the strength to do so with courage and a determined spirit. I embrace this season of purging. Help me deal

with the old, familiar territories I may have to revisit. As I put complete trust in You, help me stay the course no matter how long it may take. All these things I pray in Jesus' name.
Amen!

"Being confident of this very thing, that he which hath begun a good work in you will perform it until the day of Jesus Christ."
Philippians 1:6

Exercise 8

Are you in your wilderness? If so, what are some battles or situations you're facing? Allow God to minister to you during this time. Write down the areas the enemy is attacking. Give them to God. Ask Him to give you instructions on how you should handle them. As He answers, write them next to that area of need as a reminder of God's word.

1._____

_____

_____

_____

_____

_____

2._____

_____

_____

_____

_____

_____

3._____

_____

_____

_____

_____

_____

4._____

_____

_____

_____

_____

_____

5._____

_____

_____

_____

_____

Chapter Nine

BECOMING

I was born in the wilderness. I formed an intimate relationship with God there and began to see myself through His eyes. No longer did I have to be afraid or ashamed, I accepted that I would not always fit in. I could not have embraced this person before. I'm loving who I've become. Of course, the transformation didn't happen overnight. I was dealing with thirty-three years of bad seeds that had to be uprooted. There was a cost, but I happily paid. Now, I'm experiencing a freedom I have never known. No more sleepless nights, no more crying my eyes out and no more unnecessary hurting. God is doing a new thing in me.

Some people fight all their lives to walk in a false sense of peace, but it is nothing like the real thing. While God led me on this journey, He taught me to completely rest in Him. I know what it feels like to act like you are free and still be in bondage. His love made me understand, I didn't have to hide from my calling. The shackles which kept me bound for so long fell from my neck. No more being misunderstood and no more attaching myself to things and people for acceptance. God confirmed me through troubles. This is my time to be free.

It was often hard, and embarrassing at times, to deal with the

Tamisha God was breaking down. However, having the microscope turned in my direction delivered me. What do you do when you find yourself in this place? You stand tall, that's what you do. Don't take life personally. People have their own issues to sort out. I understood I was where God wanted me to be. It took many hard lessons and hurt feelings, but the message would become clear. It was then I was able to navigate smoothly. I found strength in not letting the world see everything I was feeling. The more I depended on God to lead me, the less I became afraid of the journey.

"And lo a voice from heaven, saying, this is my
beloved Son, in whom I am well pleased."
Matthew 3:17

We all have a purpose to bless the world in some way. We're predestined to plant seeds and everyone must tend to their own harvest. My journey was not about others. I stopped focusing on those who abandoned or betrayed me along the way and put my focus on the One who never left me. I was once asked, "If you could write your younger self and give her words of wisdom, what would they be?" I simply said, "I would tell her to trust God and form a relationship with Him." I was introduced to Him as a child but strayed as I got older. I could have avoided a lot of what I went through.

The little girl who haunted me for so long would have been put to rest. The hurt woman who got married and almost made a mess of it would have been made whole. Shattered relationships could have been saved. I'm not saying there wouldn't have been shortcomings, but I would have been better prepared to handle them. Through my experiences, my confidence grew in ways that surprised me. I no longer looked for validation from people.

I know some of you reading this book are wondering what a relationship with God looks like, or you may be asking, *how do I form a relationship with Him?* Acknowledging who you are to Him is the first step to healing. He loves you. He knows everything about you. Shouldn't He just do the work in me then, if He already knows what is going on? That sounds logical; however, God is a gentleman. He waits for your permission to intervene in your life. You will never discover your greater strength if He handed everything to you. All you need to do is become vulnerable and surrender. Don't make it hard.

Think about it. When we become vulnerable before God, we are saying, "I trust you," and intimacy begins. We all have that one best friend we can confide in, the one we feel completely comfortable telling our hurts and painful secrets. Imagine telling those secrets to the only person who can do something about them. Our friends only listen and give their advice, but God gives sound wisdom. He is the only one who heals and delivers us from the hurt we experience. Make Him your ultimate friend. He wants to be the first person you run to when you need love and comfort.

I used to confide wholeheartedly in my friends, but as much as they loved me, God loved me more and He knew what to do with my situation. I had been confiding in everyone but Him. After I surrendered completely, He began to trust me with some things He had for me. He taught me how to become my best self.

I want to share three things that brought me from only experiencing God to having a real connection with Him. First, He taught me how to pray. Prayer is direct communication between you and your Heavenly Father. It's a dialogue. As you pray, He aligns your words to His heart and your prayer life opens His purpose for your life. I have heard some people say, "I don't know how to pray or what to say." The answer? Pray what is in your heart. I told Him my problems and asked for help. I would talk to Him while driving, walking, or even during other daily activities. I knew if I just talked with Him, He would teach me how to do the rest. I didn't have to think about what I was going to say, it just flowed. A committed prayer time keeps us focused on the Lord; it becomes our guide because it leads us to a fruitful life. You must form a daily prayer life with God. You can't afford to not pray.

Secondly, God gave me a desire to start fasting. Before the mighty men and women in the Bible faced a great challenge, they fasted. Fasting is abstaining from all or some kinds of food or drink, especially as a religious observance. I was a senior in high school when I was first introduced to fasting by a young man in my class. He told me people fasted when they wanted something from God. Although I was ignorant of what he was saying, I had a need. The way I saw it, I wanted something from God then I'd better stop eating.

Before I knew it, I had gone cold turkey, no food for a whole seven days. Little did I know, he'd introduced me to something which would later become my best weapon against the enemy. Even in my ignorance, God granted my requests because my heart was pure in my petitions. Some believe fasting is not necessary in these times. I am here to tell you, it is.

As you walk closely with God, He will direct you when and how He wants you to fast. I got some of my life-changing breakthroughs after fasting. I don't know how I would have made it if I had not "turned over" my plate. It is essential to daily living. When we fast, God shows up in amazing and unexpected ways. Great strength comes right after a fast. It is unfortunate fasting is not taught in some of today's churches.

All things need practice. There were many times I failed, but I didn't give up. Fasting takes a lot of discipline, the flesh wants what it wants and if it is deprived, it will act up. There are many benefits to fasting. 1) You form a more intimate bond with God. 2) As you fast, you are preparing your body to rest, in doing so, it becomes less active which puts you in a position to hear God more clearly.

I spent a lot of time fasting and praying over the course of the last few years. There were so many attacks, I had no other choice. If not for the Lord, I would have lost my mind, literally. Fasting guards you during attacks. I was fighting spiritual battles, so I needed spiritual weapons.

It was no coincidence I was introduced to fasting at such an early age. God knew in due season I would eventually return to it. It has been my greatest asset. My experience with fasting left an impression on my heart. It was God power. He knew even if I didn't understand it, I would be bold enough to try it. I am glad I did.

Finally, of all the spiritual weapons of choice, the Bible is most powerful. If you really want to silence the enemy, hit him with the word of God. It convicts and delivers. There are many times it has cut me like a two-edged sword. It sliced me going in but healed me coming out. The enemy can't stand against the word of God. Fasting and praying are essential tools but coupled with reading the word of God, you are a supernatural bomb ready to detonate in the enemies' territory.

Satan knows the word of God, which is why he comes against us hard as we try to search it. His main goal is to keep us distracted so we don't often read it. How many times have you fallen asleep while reading the Bible? I will be the first to raise my hand. You are wide awake but as soon as you start to read the first chapter, you start dozing. Keep reading.

There is hidden treasure in the word of God. The more we seek it, the richer we become. It is your guide for every situation in your life. There are many examples in the Bible which have gotten me through difficult moments. The Word penetrates the heart of its reader. Become familiar with it, it will change you from the inside out. Just like our bodies need natural food to survive, our spirits need spiritual food. Sure, fasting and praying give you results, but the Word constantly replenishes you.

To birth my purpose, I had to search God's word for complete deliverance. I must admit, I was not an avid Bible reader and I was far from being a scholar. However, I knew it was important to make it part of my daily walk. God placed the desire for His word in my heart. Flesh resisted it strongly, but my spirit craved it. I read daily it, even if it was only for thirty minutes. If we allow, it leads us to a life of complete wholeness and joy.

Get acquainted with your Bible. If you haven't read it in a while, dust it off and become familiar again. As you read, your life will change. I would have to write another book to go into all the experiences where I've had to apply its principles. I found the peace I had been yearning for after I incorporated them into my life regularly. Before then, it was chaos and confusion. Use these three powerful spiritual tools often. Since they have become an important part of me, I dare not separate myself from them.

What God birthed out of me took time to develop. I am not the same individual who went into the wilderness, in fact, I am not even the same as I was at the beginning stages of this book. I've accepted the fact that I'm the person God is looking for. I have what it takes to birth every vision He's given me. The word of God proved me, fasting strengthened me and prayer changed me. They helped activate all it took to birth my future. Now that I am in the proper armor, I can better protect the vision.

I am a woman of substance, resilience, and strength. It took a lot of labor pains to value the work God has done in me. With every blow, came might, with every kick came power, and with every push came durability. They say only the strong survive. I must be amongst the strongest women there are because here I am. God made a champion out of me through the struggle. My dark times made me a warrior. What the enemy meant for bad, God turned around for my good.

As I leave you with these last few words, I hope my experience has been a help and a blessing. I want you to know you are not alone. I too have been scarred by many wounds, but God healed them all. Embrace every season you are in, even your seasons of struggle. They will make you better and more resilient. You are good enough and your future is bright. Smile butterfly and take flight, because what was meant to kill you, built you. Look at you now, you made it! Now go ahead and birth the vision God has given you. Become the woman He called you to be. She is waiting for you. Until we meet again! I love you, ladies.

Deliverance Prayer

Father, I thank You for the women who decided to read this book. I pray You heal every hurt and touch every situation which has left them wounded. You are a healer and Your love proves true to those who trust You. Thank You for already meeting every need and working out every situation. We declare that after today they will never be the same. I believe for full restoration in all areas which need to be restored. I plead the blood over these ladies. As they draw closer to You, I pray they encounter a relationship that will change them forever. I believe for supernatural favor over them as they become the women You created them to be. Get complete glory from their lives. All these things we pray in your precious name. Amen!

Exercise 9

You made it. You're at the finish line and I am so glad you are on your way to enjoying your best life. God has much in store for you and I believe you will get it. Take this time to write down some things you need God to birth out of you during this season. Write the vision and make it plain. This is your season of freedom. Get READY!!!

1._____

_____

_____

_____

_____

_____

2._____

_____

_____

_____

_____

_____

3._____

_____

_____

_____

_____

_____

4._____

_____

_____

_____

_____

_____

5._____

_____

_____

_____

_____

_____

NOTES

[1]https://www.guinnessworldrecords.com/world-records/tallest-tree-living/

[2]https://www.thainationalparks.com/species/ophiophagus-hannah

Visit www.anointedtosuffer for more information

Follow on Social Media
facebook.com/anointedtosuffer

ABOUT THE AUTHOR

If you saw Tamisha McQueen, you might say she has fire in her eyes. There is a fierce determination to not only survive but to succeed against all odds.

She is a wife, mother, entrepreneur and motivational speaker. Childhood trauma exposed her to great suffering but eventually created a passion to see other women delivered and set free. She lives in Florida with her husband and daughter.

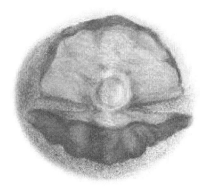

"In order to mold His people, God often has to melt them"
Amish Proverb

AFFIRMATIONS

Write Your Affirmations Here.

AFFIRMATIONS

Write Your Affirmations Here.

AFFIRMATIONS

Write Your Affirmations Here.

AFFIRMATIONS

Write Your Affirmations Here.

_____

_____

_____

_____

_____

_____

_____

_____

_____

_____

_____

AFFIRMATIONS

Write Your Affirmations Here.

_____

_____

_____

_____

_____

_____

_____

_____

_____

_____

_____

Made in the USA
Coppell, TX
25 March 2020

17627626R00060